Introduction

There is something magical about poetry. The memory clings to it more tightly than to prose, and often the slightest allusion will recall a verse, stanza, or entire poem from the vague mists of a forgotten past. To train their memories Victorian children recited poems of increasing length and complexity as they grew, and by the time they reached adulthood poetry itself was such a comfortable friend to them that popular games involved making up verses on the spot or reciting poems backwards (from memory!) while a crowd of giggling friends attempted distractions. From the humdrum to the sacred, poetry permeated life. It was used for every purpose from selling corsets to exalting the divine —and, as it has been since time immemorial, it was used to make love. Victorian love poetry ranges from poignant little peeps at simple couples whose only wealth was their devotion to sublime praise of love immortal. When we read the poetry of the Victorians we feel our own hearts quicken as we share their intimacies.

Details of life change over time but certain elements are constants of the human condition: love is the most beautiful of all of these. There is a sweet familiarity to the description of a heart thrilling at a beloved's touch, no matter where or when the lovers may be meeting. At the same time, each love is uniquely its own. The precise way it blossoms depends on the lovers' personalities and their stations in life. It is appropriate that English speakers often compare love to honey: it is always sweet yet the subtle notes of that sweetness are flavored in different ways by the flowers from which the nectar is drawn. Honey gathered exclusively from blackberry blossoms has a distinct tang, while honey drawn from roses tastes of the queen of flowers. The richest honey combines the flavors of many blooms, and this choice collection of poetry takes a lesson from the bees. Shy maidens and coquettes, eloquent gentlemen and simple lads of rough education but pure hearts all play their part here, and the language of each poem is a reflection of the sweethearts' personalities.

The volume opens, appropriately enough, with the story of a love token which has lain long buried, and which is then unearthed and marvelled at by later generations. From there the collection follows the course of love itself, from the first shy and timid glances to the deep devotion of wedded bliss. It is not an overly large book, but then I always felt that a book of love poetry should be small enough to hold close to the heart. It is love itself which fills the world.

—Sarah A. Chrisman

Bessie's Answer

Tell me, Bessie, if you love me,
    I would dearly like to know;
And if you do, then, may I ask you,
    Why you always shun me so?

Not a word? You will not even
    Lift your downcast eyes to mine,
Since no single word you give me—
    Why avert those eyes of thine?

Does my suit deserve such answer,
    That no other you will give
Than these sly, averted glances?
    Then, it's freedom—pray, forgive?

If 'tis scorn that keeps you silent,
    Or kind pity veils your eyes;
Then; but since 'tis plain that nothing
    In your heart to mine replies.

But 'tis past; my dream is over!
    I am going far away,
Since you cannot bid me love you,
    It were madness here to stay.

But, how much I love you, darling,

You will never, never know;
Since no words of mine can tell you,
And no act may ever show.

How! what mean you, Bessie darling?
You relent; you bid me stay;
You're not cruel; do not mock me—
Can you love me, Bessie, say?

Love you, Willie! I have loved you,
Oh, so long; but do you know,
Until plain you said you loved me,
I—I couldn't—tell you so.

—Elizabeth Benton
Peterson's Magazine, September, 1877, p. 200.

A Face So Fair

Speak! Let me hear the music of thy voice
Those lips so eloquent! O let them part,
And tell me of the light within those eyes,
From which such glowing beams of magic
dart.
Sure on thy trembling lips such sweet
thoughts play
As only Love himself imprinted there;
And in thine eyes shines a celestial ray,
Caught from the radiance of some vision fair.
Sweet lips, frank eyes, and chin with grace so
molded
As the fresh petal of a flower new-blown;
And thy fair brow by golden clouds infolded,
As bright aurora 'cross the sky is thrown.
O that thou wouldst to me thy secrets tell,
For in a face so fair must sweet thoughts
dwell.

—Andrew B. Dick
The Cosmopolitan. May, 1898, p. 111.

Brown Eyes and Blue

Under the shade of the sheltering vines,
They met, at the close of day;
She fresh from the dairy, clean and sweet,
And he from the field of hay.
She had brown eyes, and a gentle smile,
Brown eyes that were tender and true;
And he, a manly and graceful form,
And eyes that were bold and blue.

They spoke of the dairy, fresh and sweet,
They talked of the field of hay;
But the maiden's heart beat quick and fast,
For she knew what he'd come to say.
The moon shone out with a clear, soft light,
Blue eyes looked into the brown,
And the youth could read a world of bliss
In the maiden's eyes, cast down.

Under the shade of the sheltering vines,
His arm stole around her waist;
But the words that he spoke in her listening
ear,
Have never with pen been traced;
For the moon went under a fleecy cloud,
And veiled from her eyes the sight;
And only the stars, and the maiden's heart,

Could tell what he said that night.

—Nannie Sadler
Peterson's Magazine, May, 1877, p. 363.

Love's Messenger

Breeze from the South which softly strays
And lingers long in Nature's ways,
Whisper to her I love.

Tell her that I am coming too,
Tell her when fields and woods do woo,
And skies are blue above,
My heart unto hers will sweetly sing,
And the melody through her life shall ring.

—Nina Picton
Good Housekeeping, July 20, 1889. p. 152.

My Ideal

I ask not radiant beauty for her face,
Nor perfect contour in her cherished form;—
If but with love sincere her heart should be
warm
Each line to me will seem of matchless
grace,—
Nor care I though she lack a cultured mind
In love of bygone sages deeply learned;—
Full many a soul life's truths has well
discerned,
By pureness made an eye among the blind.—
Let her be simple, sweet, and true in heart,—
Neither too good to sense the joys of earth,
Nor yet too sordid Heaven to understand;—
With calm reliance in her soul's command,
Able by her example to impart
Her virtue to the children of her birth.

—Laurens Maynard
The Cosmopolitan. October, 1891. p. 652.

A Serious Matter

Night-blooming cereus—a single night
It glistens 'neath the moonbeams, waxen
white.
Two lovers stand beside the blossom rare;
Their love unto its beauty they compare.
(Will that love's beauty, like the flow'rs, take
flight?)

Then, turning from it, 'neath the new moon's
light,
They stroll and count the stars in heaven's
height;
They see the dog star scintillating there—
Night-blooming Sirius.

Alas, poor youth! His is enamoured quite.
He longs to tell her of his love; but fright
Doth lock the speech with which he would
declare
His mingled hope, affection, and despair.
He is a—you would say so, at first sight—
Knight "blooming" serious.

—Harry B. Smith
America, May 23, 1889. p. 245.

The Little Telltale

Once, on a golden afternoon,
With radiant faces and hearts in tune,
Two fond lovers in dreaming mood
Threaded a rural solitude.
Wholly happy, they only knew
That the earth was bright and the sky was
blue;
That light and beauty and joy and song
Charm'd the ways they pass'd along:
The air was fragrant with woodland scents;
The squirrel frisk'd on the roadside fence;
And hovering near them, "chee, chee, chink?"
Queried the curious bobolink.
Pausing and peering with sidelong head,
As saucily questioning all they said;
While the ox-eye danced on its slender stem,
And all glad Nature rejoiced with them.
Over the odorous fields were strown
Wilting windrows of grass new-mown,
And rosy billows of clover bloom
Surged in the sunshine and breathed perfume.
Swinging low on a slender limb,
The sparrow warbled his wedding hymn;
And, balancing on a blackberry brier,
The bobolink sang with his heart on fire,—

"Chink! If you wish to kiss her, do!
Do it, do it! You coward, you!
Kiss her! Kiss, kiss her! Who will see?
Only we three! we three! we three!"

Under garlands of drooping vines,
Through dim vistas of sweet-breathed pines,
Past wide meadow-fields lately mow'd,
Wander'd the indolent country road.
The lovers follow'd it, listening still,
And, loitering slowly, as lovers will,
Enter'd a low-roof'd bridge, that lay,
Dusky and cool, in their pleasant way.
Under its arch a smooth, bright stream
Silently glided, with glint and gleam,
Shaded by graceful elms that spread
Their verdurous canopy overhead,—
The stream so narrow, the boughs so wide,
They met and mingled across the tide.
Alders loved it, and seem'd to keep
Patient watch as it lay asleep,
Mirroring clearly the trees and sky
And the flitting form of the dragon-fly,
Save where the swift-wing'd swallow play'd
In and out in the sun and shade,
And, darting and circling in merry chase,
Dipp'd, and dimpled its clear dark face.

Fluttering lightly from brink to brink

A Floral Flirtation

In the garden were leisurely walking,
Brave Robin and Roxy the fair,
And Robin, while walking and talking,
Twined roses in Roxy's brown hair;

Rosebuds and roses all blushing,
With sprigs of the sweet mignonette.
While the blood to their faces kept rushing,
When Robin's eyes Roxy's eyes met;

Jasmine, Laburnum, and Larkspur;
Verbenas, deep dyed and pale,
Gay pansies and Lilies of th' Valley
Heard Love tell his stammering tale;

While the lovers kept walking and talking--
Four eyes bent down to the ground;
Two hearts had been lost, they discovered,
And then discovered them—found.

But didn't know what to do with them,
The lost and found hearts—for a while,
So each plucked a new and fresh nosegay,
And each gave the other a smile.

Each a stem of Forget-me-not gathered,
And each said "Take and keep this;"
Their vows thus exchanged with fresh

flowers,
They sealed the exchange—with a kiss;

Fidelity, secrecy, silence,
Each promised to faithfully hold,
Till Robin could earn for his Roxy
A home, and some shekels of gold.

But alas, some open-eared listeners--
Winged messengers, hurrying by,
Saw what had been done in the garden,
And tattled to earth and to sky;

"Oh! Robin and Roxy are lovers,"
They piped with a song and a shout,
"And have plighted their troth in the garden,"
—So the delicate secret was out.

The world soon had the whole story
Which Robin could not deny,
And Roxy, when bantered about it,
Blushed back 'neath a mischievous eye.

So Cupid, and Robin, and Roxy,
Made love, with flowers for words,
As they walked and talked in the garden,
And nobody told but the birds.

—The American Gardener
Good Housekeeping May 11, 1889, p. 24.

The Merriest Girl That's Out

With laughter and good humor, why,
I pass my time away,
So, while I'm here I'll do my best
To please you with my lay.
Then come along and join my song,
And raise a merry shout,
To welcome me, for I'm, you see,
The merriest girl that's out.

Now then, young men,
Don't be melancholy,
Just see, like me,
If you can't be jolly.
If any thing goes wrong with me,
I never sulk or pout:
In fact I am, and always was,
The merriest girl that's out.

The gentlemen complain and say,
I'm such a dreadful flirt;
But if they make love to me,
Their hearts I'm sure to hurt—
I really can't help laughing,
When I hear them sigh about,
For sentiment it don't suit me,
I'm the merriest girl that's out.

Now then, young men,
Don't be melancholy,
Just see, like me,
If you can't be jolly.
If any thing goes wrong with me,
I never sulk or pout:
In fact I am, and always was,
The merriest girl that's out.

The notes and presents I receive
Would fill a basket quite,
While bouquets rare, I do declare,
Are sent to me every night.
The notes all speak of broken hearts,
Some means it, I've no doubt;
I'm sorry, yet I still remain
The merriest girl that's out.

Now then, young men,
Don't be melancholy,
Just see, like me,
If you can't be jolly.
If any thing goes wrong with me,
I never sulk or pout:
In fact I am, and always was,
The merriest girl that's out.

—Anonymous
Home Songster, 1883. pp. 79—80.

Base-ball of Life

How much a society girl's life resembles
A game of base-ball in the fair field of life;
Her friends, on the judgement stand, eager
assemble,
To witness the victory or triumph the strife.

The game has been called and reluctantly
entered;
She knows all are watching her heart play—
the ball—
Yet none know just where the attraction is
centred,
Or even on whom the rich treasure will fall.

The nine who are playing with hearts all afire,
In hopes that opponents defeated return,
Resemble the number of those who aspire
To the hand for which many incessant will
yearn.

The first base is he who has won by endeavor
Some token of friendship above all the rest;
The second base, he who for love's sake will
weather
E'en love's competition—the fortress to test.

Third base is the man who, in spite of desire
To conquer his passion, must yield to the
charm;
Still watches the heart-ball as higher and
higher
It rises—then falls—in another man's palm.

Short-stop's the man who is furthest from
winning,
And yet he is nearer the pitcher, 'tis true;
He eagerly watches the heart-ball while
spinning—
In somebody's heaven—and *he* becomes blue.

Throughout the whole poem that heart's been
ascending,
Far into man's heaven, expanding so wide;
But now it has changed and downward
descending,
It falls to the catcher! Who is he? Decide!

—J. Adele Mulligan
America, April 25, 1889. p. 115.

My Lady Disdain

"What, my dear Lady Disdain, are you still
living?" —*Shakespeare*.

She's a sweet little damsel of twenty,
A mixture of sadness and fun,
Of lovers I know she has plenty,
This sorrowful rhymer is one.
If only on me she'd take pity,
My highest delight I'd attain,
For I'm but a clerk in the city;
And she is—my Lady Disdain.

I know very well she's above me,
As far as the sun or the moon;
To think such an angel could love me,
Would be far too much of a boon.
If I wrote an amorous ditty,
She'd burn it I know in a flame;
For I'm but a clerk in the city,
And she is—my Lady Disdain.

I dream of her while I am writing,
Or poring o'er some legal flaw;
My future career she is blighting,
I love her instead of the law;
No knowledge from Coke or from Chitty,

This rhymer is able to gain;
For I'm but a clerk in the city,
And she is—my Lady Disdain.

Alas! if I only had money,
A couple of thousand a year;
To me she'd be sweeter than honey,
Nor think that my manners were queer;
If I were but handsome and witty,
Beside her I'd always remain,
But I'm but a clerk in the city,
And she is—my Lady Disdain.

I know this sweet dreaming is idle,
Her beauty I never can claim,
The bells ring aloud for her bridal,
With one who has riches and fame;
But she is so dainty and pretty,
That queen of my heart she must reign,
Tho' I'm but a clerk in the city,
And she is—my Lady Disdain.

—F.W. Hume
Good Housekeeping, June 12, 1886, p. 83.

Kismet

Relentless fate pursues us all
And fills our hearts with folly;
For I love you, and you love John,
And John loves distant Molly.

But Moll adores the dashing Frank,
Whose thoughts to Sallie wander;
Nor can sweet Sallie once forget
The eyes of Charlie yonder;

While Charlie bends his gaze on Nell,
Who swears she loves me only;
And thus the circle grows complete
Wherein each heart is lonely.

Now, should you turn and love but me,
And John win lovely Molly,
Shall Sall love Frank and Nell love Charles,—
Say, how can that be folly?

—Arthur Fairfax
The New England Magazine, May, 1895. p. 384.

Mignonette

I passed before her garden gate;
She stood among her roses,
And stooped a little from the state
In which her pride reposes,
To make her flowers a graceful plea
For luring and delaying me.

"When summer blossoms fade so soon,"
She said with winning sweetness,
"Who does not wear the badge of June
Lacks something of completeness.
My garden welcomes you to-day,
Come in and gather, while you may."

I entered in: she led me through
A maze of leafy arches,
Where velvet-purple pansies grew
Beneath the sighing larches,—
A shadowy, still, and cool retreat
That gave excuse for lingering feet.

She paused; pulled down a trailing vine;
And twisted round her finger
Its starry sprays of jessamine,
As one who seeks to linger.
But I smiled lightly in her face,

And passed on to the open space.

Passed many a flower-bed fitly set
In trim and blooming order,
And plucked at last some mignonette
That strayed along the border;
A simple thing that had no bloom,
And but a faint and fair perfume.

She wondered why I would not choose
That dreamy amaryllis,—
"And could I really, then, refuse
Those heavenly white lilies!
And leave ungathered on the slope
This passion-breathing heliotrope?"

She did not know—what need to tell
So fair and fine a creature?—
That there was one who loved me well
Of widely different nature;
A little maid whose tender youth,
And innocence, and simple truth,

Had won my heart with qualities
That far surpassed her beauty,
And held me with unconscious ease
Enthralled of love and duty;
Whose modest graces all were met
And symboled in my mignonette.

I passed outside her garden gate,
And left her proudly smiling;
Her roses bloomed too late, too late
She saw, for my beguiling,
I wore instead —and wear it yet—
The single spray of mignonette.

Its fragrance greets me unaware,
A vision clear recalling
Of shy, sweet eyes, and drooping hair
In girlish tresses falling,
And little hands so white and fine
That timidly creep into mine;

As she —ignorant of the arts
That wiser maids are plying—
Has crept into my heart of hearts
Past doubting or denying;
Therein, while suns shall rise and set,
To bloom unchanged, my Mignonette!

—Mary Bradley
Hill's Manual of Social and Business Forms,
Chicago: Hill Standard Book Co., 1891. p. 560.

A Valentine

Beware of one who loves thee but too well!
Of one who fain would bind thee with a spell,
With power to draw thee, as an unknown land
Lures the impassioned traveler to its strand.
Oh! if thou wouldst be free,
Beware of me!

Beware of eyes that softly fix on thee,
Tamed in their restless glances by thine own,
And of a voice, where all things that may be
In maiden hearts are told in every tone.
If thou wouldst still be free,
Beware of me!

But if a longing, born within thy soul
Gives thee a far off glimpse of unknown bliss,
Then let thy love speed onward to its goal,
Nor thy true rest and joy for blindness miss.
If thou wouldst not be free,
Then come to me!

—Anonymous
Scribner's, February, 1880, p. 593.

A Quarrel

It's over; and we're strangers now!
These years of love count nothing, then?
And you take back each heart-warm vow,
And throw me back my vows again?

What did you say—what did I do?
What did you do—what did I say?
And which began it—I or you?
What does it matter, anyway?

We two, to part for a hard thought,
A bitter word—repented—see—
When the whole world can give us naught
If I lose you—and you lose me!

Think of our past, the days like flowers,
Which still to memory lend due grace,
Think of the future—sunless hours
When I should never see your face.

Think of the present. What is done
Is done—but oh—forgive—forget!
Thank God—who meant us two for one,
We have not lost each other yet!

—E. Nesbit
The Leisure Hour, 1891, p. 156.

The End of the Quarrel

He kept his vow of absence well--
For two whole days together!
But when the second twilight fell,
Love broke the tightened tether. The chilly
evening flung its rain,
With peevish gust and sprinkle;
To threaten, through the glimmering pane,
The firebrand's fitful twinkle. But when a
sudden rush of air
Blew out the lighted candle,
She, looking not, was still aware
What fingers turned the handle. How could he
guess the level lid
Some secret tears dissembled?
Or that her silence proudly chid
The tones that would have trembled? So,
doubtful, angry, half-ashamed,
Half pleased to have defied her,
He took the chair the cat had claimed,
And, speechless, sat beside her! The rusty
clock-hand slowly creaked
From minute on to minute;
A mouse from out the shadow squeaked,
Nor stirred the quiet in it; The flickering
firelight seemed to rise
And grow to wall and rafter,

While lips that trembled once with sighs
Were trembling now with laughter; Till, spent
at last, the sleepy brand
Looked at each silent lover,
Blinked thrice, and left them hand in hand
Beneath the darkness' cover!

—Kate Putnam Osgood
Good Housekeeping, June 1892, p. 277.

Courtship

Setting the Table

With cheeks like the rose that in summer-time
grows
In the old-fashioned garden at home,
With eyes like twin wells and black hair that
tells
Curly treason to hair-pin and comb.

With footsteps as light and with apron as
white
As the foam on a wave o' the sea,
Bonny sweet Mabel was setting the table,
Was setting the table for tea.

While John by the window was talking with
dad
About witch-grass and staples and rings,
Of lumber and teams while his honest heart
dreams
A fond dream of far different things.

For John had come over to ask neighbor
Brown
For the loan of a plow, but his hat
And his Sunday coat took a brush far remote
From an every-day errand like that.

And still on the subject of lumber and teams
With dad's view he is fain to agree,
But he wonders meanwhile if Mabel's sweet
smile
Presages a bidding to tea.

And when for a moment they left him alone
With the table, the tea and the cat,
To settle his doubt it was quickly found out
What this amorous swain would be at.

With fish-rod and hook from the neighboring
brook
And its wild piscatorial joys,
In a moment more to the half-open door
Came the farmer's two tow-headed boys.

The foremost looked in, then he turned with a
grin
And he whispered "As sure as the fates,
Look Bill by hooky, I'll bet you a cookie
That the great spoon is *counting the plates*."

Last night 'twas my fate to be walking quite
late
Past John's modest house in the lane,
The kitchen was near and the story quite
clear,
That the lamplight had told on the pane.

From the stove and the cat to the rocker and
mat
All things looked suspiciously new,
And being sweet Mabel was setting the table,
Was setting the table for *two*.

—Alice O. Darling
Good Housekeeping, January 18, 1889, p. 138.

An Invitation

O Come into the garden, sweet,
At dawn of day, at dawn of day;
For Love has the key of the postern-gate,
Make no delay! make no delay!

Here's beds of roses white and red,
Where softly shall you fare,
Here's crowds of yellow marigolds
To deck your shining hair.

Here's meadow lawns and grassy plots,
Where dainty feet may stray,
Here's doves to coo, and birds to sing
Love's tender roundelay.

Here's peaches from the southern wall,
O sweetheart, taste and try,
Here's arbors green and trellises
To kiss, and no one by.

And all these things await you, love,
At dawn of day, at dawn of day;
For Love is here with song and lute.
Make no delay! make no delay!

—Anonymous
Scribner's, April, 1880, p. 897.

Fairy-Belle

The pride of the village, and the fairest in the
dell,
Is the queen of my song, and her name is
Fairy-Belle;
The sound of her light step may be heard
upon the hill,
Like the fall of the snow-drop, or the dripping
of the rill.

Fairy-Belle, gentle Fairy-Belle,
The star of the night and the lily of the day,
Fairy-Belle, the queen of all the dell,
Long may she revel on her bright sunny way.

She sighs to the meadows, and she carols to
the streams,
She laughs in the sunlight, and smiles while in
her dreams,
Her hair, like the thistle-down, is borne upon
the air,
And her heart, like the humming-bird's, is free
from ev'ry care.

Her soft notes of melody around me sweetly
fall;
Her eye full of love, is now beaming on my

soul;
The sound of that gentle voice, the glance of
that eye,
Surround me with rapture that no other heart
could sigh.

—Anonymous
Home Songster, 1883. pp. 23—24.

What She Told Me At The Gate

'Tis every night at sunset,
I wander forth to meet
The fairy little damsel
Who comes with smiles to greet;
Her face is like the sunshine,
Her beauty is my fate,
For she always looks so charming
When she meets me at the gate.

She meets me, she greets me,
She is my bonnie Sue;
And what she told me at the gate,
Ah! don't you wish you knew?

And if you hear I'm married,
And settled down in life,
You'll know I have no other
Than Susie for my wife.
Last night she promised something
I must not here relate,
For oh, I cannot tell you
What she told me at the gate.

She meets me, she greets me,
She is my bonnie Sue;
But what she told me at the gate,

Was—Don't you wish you knew?

—D. Sherman
Peterson's Magazine, 1877, p. 441.

Love's Eloquence

In dreams of thee I feel the eloquence
That floods the souls of poets half divine;
Earth blooms anew, and music makes a sense
Of glorious pain, and thought gives warmth
like wine.

Oh, to give this to language! to distil
With wizardry the heavenly vapor fleet
And in a word, a gem, a flower, at will,
Cast it in trembling passion at thy feet.

—Thomas Walsh
The Cosmopolitan, April, 1900, p. 684.

The Trysting Place

Where the milk-white lilies grow,
Each pure chalice gleaming whitely,
When the moon is shining brightly,
Comes my darling, treading lightly,
Where the milk-white lilies grow.
Yet, not long, the maiden lingers
Where the milk-white lilies grow.

Where the royal roses bloom,
In their robes of crimson splendor,
And their balmy sweetness squander,
There my love delights to wander,
Where the royal roses bloom.
Yet, not long, the dear one tarries,
Where the royal roses bloom.

Where the humble violet bends,
In the midst of snow-white clover,
'Neath the oak-trees' leafy cover,
There my darling meets her lover,
Where the humble violet bends.
There I meet my heart's dear treasure,
Where the humble violet bends.

—Katie Higgins
Peterson's Magazine, 1877, p. 300.

You Kissed Me

You kissed me! My head dropped low on
your breast,
With a feeling of shelter and infinite rest;
While the holy emotions my tongue dare not
speak
Flashed up in a flame from my heart to my
cheek.
Your arms held me fast—oh, your arms were
so bold!
Heart beat against heart in your passionate
fold.
Your glances seemed drawing my soul
through my eyes,
As the sun draws the mist from the seas to the
skies.
Your lips clung to mine, till I prayed in my
bliss,
They might never unclasp from the rapturous
kiss.

You kissed me! My heart and my breath and
my will,
In delirious joy, for a moment stood still,
Life had for me then no temptations, no
charms,
No vision of happiness outside your arms.

And were I this instant an angel, posessed,
Of the peace and the joy that are given the
blest,
I would fling my white robe unrepentingly
down,
I would tear from my forehead its beautiful
crown,
To nestle once more in that haven of rest,
Your lips upon mine, and my head on your
breast.

You kissed me! My soul, in a bliss so divine,
Reeled and swooned like a drunken man
foolish with wine;
And I thought 'twere delicious to die there, if
death
Would come while my lips were yet moist
with your breath;
If my pulses would stop, if my heart might
grow cold
While your arms clasped me round in their
passionate fold,
And these are the questions I ask day and
night:
Must my lips taste no more such exquisite
delight?
Would you care if your breast were my shelter
as then?

And if you were here—would you kiss me
again?

—Josephine H. Hunt
Peterson's Magazine, June, 1883, p. 472.

What Will You Do, Love?

"What will you do, love, when I am going
With white sail flowing, the seas beyond?
What will you do, love, when waves divide
us,
And friends may chide us for being fond?"

"Tho' waves divide us, and friends be chiding,
In faith abiding, I'll still be true;
And I'll pray for thee on the stormy ocean,
In deep devotion; that's what I'll do."

"What will you do, love, if distant tidings
Thy fond confidings should undermine;
And I abiding 'neath sultry skies,
Should think other eyes more bright than
thine?"

"Oh, name it not, tho' brand of shame
Were on thy name, I'd still be true;
But that heart of thine, should another share it,
I could not bear it,—what would I do?"

"What would you do, love, when home
returning,
With high hopes burning, with wealth for you,
If my bark, which bounded o'er foreign foam,

Were lost near home, ah! what would you
do?"

"So thou wert spared, I'd bless the morrow,
In want and sorrow, that left me you;
And I'd welcome thee from the wasting
billow,
This heart thy pillow; that's what I'd do."

—Samuel Lover, 1842.
Franklin-Square Song Collection, Ed. J.P. McCaskey.
New York: Harper & Brothers, 1881. p. 90.

In Absence

Can longest miles that hide thy face from me,
Can countless years, or anything that blights,
Blot from this heart the glory rare that lights
Its darkness up? I never can be free
Again from love's sweet presence. Should it be
We meet no more, I know love's cunning rites
Still, still would witch thy face where man indites.

And, as in violet-time upon the lea
The south wind blows, thy voice still from the flow'r,
The sunshine, all things fair, would speak, would call.
I know not, dear, if yet from thy fair bow'r
The birds have fled; this only, all in all,
Despite the sea between, the mounts that bar,
Its one white rose makes glad this heart afar.

—Chapman, J. Warren.
Peterson's Magazine, January, 1883, p. 54.

Nocturne

Here, at the garden gate,
In the dusk and dew,
Under the stars I wait
For my sweetheart true;
Here is the trysting place,
Here I shall see her face,
Like a lily bloom
In the fragrant gloom,
Marvel of light and grace!

Softly the leaves above,
In the winds that blow,
Whisper of her I love
While I linger so;
Dreaming, I linger here
Under the starlight clear,
Till the wind goes by
With a joyous sigh,
Telling me she is near!

Hark, on the grass how light
Fall her footsteps now!
See—like the crescent white
Of the moon—her brow!
Under the stars alone,
Hither my sweet has flown;

She is here at last,
And her heart beats fast,
Happy against my own!

—Frank Dempster Sherman
The Cosmopolitan, January, 1891, p. 350.

Courtship

It chanced, they say, upon a day,
A furlong from the town,
That she was strolling up the way
As he was strolling down—
She humming low, as might be so,
A ditty sweet and small;
He whistling loud a tune, you know,
That had no tune at all.
It happened so—precisely so—
As all their friends and neighbors know.

As I and you perhaps might do,
They gazed upon the ground;
But when they'd gone a yard or two
Of course they both looked round.
They both were pained; they both explained
What caused their eyes to roam;
And nothing after that remained
But he should see her home.
It happened so—precisely so—
As all their friends and neighbors know.

Next day to that 'twas common chat,
Admitting no debate,
A bonnet close beside a hat
Was sitting on a gate.

A month, not more, had bustled o'er,
When braving nod and smile,
One blushing soul came through the door
Where two went up the aisle.
It happened so—precisely so—
As all their friends and neighbors know.

—Frederick Langbridge
Peterson's Magazine, March, 1883, p. 234.

Grandmother Sees

Grandmother's knitting has lost its charm;
Unheeded it lies in her ample lap,
While the sunset's crimson, soft and warm,
Touches the frills of her snowy cap.

She is gazing on two beside the bars,
Under the maple,—who little care
For the growing dusk, or the rising stars,
Or the hint of frost in the autumn air.

One is a tender slip of a girl,
And one a man in the pride of youth,—
The maiden pure as the purest pearl,
The lover strong in his steadfast truth.

"Sweet, my own, as a rose of June,"
He says full low o'er the golden head.
It would sound to her like a dear old tune,
Could grandmother hear the soft words said.

For it seems but a little while ago
Since under a maple, beside the bars,
She stood a girl while the sunset's glow
Melted away 'mid the evening stars.

And little you dream how fond a prayer

Goes up to God through his silver stars,
From the aged woman gazing there,
For the two who linger beside the bars.

—Margaret Sangster
The Shamrock. April 10, 1880. p. 455.

Proposals and Weddings

Pretty little Sarah, or $7 a Week

My heart is like a pumpkin, swollen big with
love
For one of the fairest girls in creation;
She is too good for me, though I am far above
The drudgery and ill-paid of my station
Her father keeps a butcher-shop on the
Harlem road;
For this little virgin, of love I've got a load,
I've spent a fortune on her; but of that I only
speak—
For, what a fortune I must have on seven
dollars a week!

Pretty little Sarah with the golden hair,
Her beauty jealous maidens will be scorning;
She ought to be an angel, and if only rich I
were,
I'd marry her so early in the morning.

The first time that I met her, 'twas in the
pouring rain,
I proferred her my arm and umbrella;
She looked with a smile; I said I'd see her
home;
She thanked me with a voice so low and
mellow.

When we arrived at home, she said, she'd ask
me in,
But her parents they were poor. Said I,
poverty's no sin.
No doubt she thinks me rich, but of course I
didn't speak—
For I was doing my heavy on seven dollars a
week.

Pretty little Sarah with the golden hair,
Her beauty jealous maidens will be scorning;
She ought to be an angel, and if only rich I
were,
I'd marry her so early in the morning.

She's got a little ankle, she's got a little foot,
And pretty little fingers running taper;
Her waist is round and small, her mouth is
best of all,
With ruby lips not twice as thick as paper;
She's always dressed in silks, her notions they
are high;
Although her figure's small, her bearing's in
the sky,
When she belongs to me, of course I never
speak,
What lots of silks she'll get from me on seven
dollars a week.

Pretty little Sarah with the golden hair,
Her beauty jealous maidens will be scorning;
She ought to be an angel, and if only rich I
were,
I'd marry her so early in the morning.

Her parents they are poor, but she's a milliner,
And earns large wages in the city:
Some she gives her mother for keep and
board,
The rest she spends to make her pretty.
She never saves a cent, though to me she says
she will;
To pay the expense of marriage is a sugar-
coated pill;
And should we have a family—but soon I
must not speak.
A wife and fourteen children on seven dollars
a week!

Pretty little Sarah with the golden hair,
Her beauty jealous maidens will be scorning;
She ought to be an angel, and if only rich I
were,
I'd marry her so early in the morning.

—Anonymous
Home Songster, 1883. pp. 60—61.

Pretty Jemima

My love she lives in a two-pair back,
Her eyes as bright as the stars of night,
Of falling in love I've got a knack,
And she's the girl for me.
At six o'clock she leaves off work,
At seven, she's finished her tea,
At eight, she's dressed in all her best,
And she comes for a walk with me.

I once was afraid to speak outright
I was so shy, I feared to try,
The thought of it put me all in a fright,
So I'd grizzle and pine all day.
I was getting as thin as a scaffold pole,
My buttons all fell away,
And just because I hadn't the nerve
To pluck up courage and say:

Oh! pretty Jemima, don't say—No!
Oh, hi oh! don't say—No.
Pretty Jemima, don't say—No.
And we will married be.

We went for a walk, not long ago—
Thinks I—somehow, I'll tell her now;
I just was going to let her know,
When she spied a milliner shop;

A hat and feathers was there for sale,
I couldn't do less than stop:
By the time I had bought it, my courage had
gone
And I couldn't the question pop.

At last, one morning, I bought the ring,
And hit on a plan to make me a man;
Thinks I to myself, this is the thing,
This night shall I cast the die.
I held it up: look ye here, I said,
The moment it caught her eye,
Her lovely cheeks were suffused with red,
And seeing no one by, I said:

Oh! pretty Jemima, don't say—No!
Oh, hi oh! don't say—No.
Pretty Jemima, don't say—No.
And we will married be.

Of course, I was anxious to know my fate,
I almost dreaded the words I said,
Whether to be with joy elate,
Or be the most wretched of men.
She tried it on her finger, and said:
'Twas a little too large, but then
I could buy a keeper, and we'd get wed
Next Saturday morning at ten.

—Anonymous
Home Songster, 1883. pp. 58—60.

Over the Banisters

Over the banisters bends a face,
Daringly sweet and beguiling;
Somebody standing in careless grace,
And watching the picture, smiling.

The light burns dim in the hall below,
Nobody sees her standing,
Saying "Good-night" again, soft and slow,
Half-way up the landing.

Nobody, only the eyes of brown,
Tender and full of meaning,
That smile on the fairest face in town,
Over the banisters leaning.

Tired and sleepy, with drooping head,
I wonder why she lingers,
And when all the good-nights are said,
Why somebody holds her fingers—

Holds her fingers and draws her down,
Suddenly growing bolder,
Till her loose hair drops in masses brown,
Like a mantle over his shoulder.

Over the banisters soft hands fair

Brush his cheeks like a feather;
Bright-brown tresses and dusky hair
Meet and mingle together.

There's a question asked, there's a swift
caress,
She has flown like a bird from the hallway;
But over the banisters drops a "Yes"
That shall brighten the world for him alway.

—Anonymous
Good Housekeeping, November 26, 1887. p. 44.

Wedding Bells Are Ringing

When all the world is melody
And sweet the wild bird's singing,
Gay Cupid bends anew his bow
For wedding bells are ringing.

When blooms the wild rose on the cliff
And lilies by the river,
And on the hillside's sunny slope
The dainty violets quiver.

Then hark! the sound adown the vale
On summer breezes springing,
A merry chime of hope and joy
The wedding bells are ringing.

The warm sun's rays, a golden key
Old Winter's ice-chains sever,
But here, to-day, a bond is formed
To link two hearts forever.

Then peal, clear bells! Ring out, sweet bells,
Love's happy message winging,
Your chime again the secret tells
Of wedding bells a ringing.

—Marienne Heaton
Good Housekeeping, June 26, 1886. p. 99.

The Bridal Dress

Oh! the rustle to it and the glisten to it!
Pray thee, listen to it.
It is white and bright, with a shimmer of light,
Like the moon on the snow on a winter's
night.
'Tis from Worth, they say.
Who is he, I pray?
There are pearls sewn over it.
And the laces which cover it—
Was there ever such lace?—like the dainty
white trace
Of the frost on the pane; of such wonderful
grace;
Was it ever woven by human hand,
Or was it the gift from a fairy's wand?
Then the orange blossoms so white and sweet,
Fit to garland my lady from head to feet.
Oh! the whiteness of it.
Oh! the brightness of it.
Yet none too white
Or none too bright.
My bride is the daintiest maid that I know,
The dearest and fairest and sweetest, I trow,
Ever told of in song or story,
Ever sung of in tales of glory.
Come weal or come woe,

Nothing fears me, my bride,
The world's before me
And I've you by my side.

—Isabel Gorden
The Cosmopolitan, August, 1891, p. 437.

A Gift

What's the best thing I can offer
As a gift for you to-day?
Any present I may proffer
You will value it, you say.
That is very sweetly spoken,
Yet, however that may be,
I should wish to choose the token
Carefully—so let us see.

Shall I send a nosegay, dearest?
Ah! the summer flowers are dead,
And the leaves are in their serest,
And the fruit has lost its red;
And, besides, the flowers would perish,
Lose their scent, and fade and die;
But a gift for *you* to cherish
Should be more than petals dry.

Shall I send a *pretty* present,
Something tasteful, something rare?
Something to the senses pleasant,
Something quaint, or something fair?
Yet, perhaps, *you* would not choose it,
If the choice could rest with you,
And some day perhaps you'd lose it,
Or the thing might break in two.

Shall I send you for your reading
Some loved book of noble thought,
Spirit-stirring, spirit-leading,
Teaching what you would be taught?
Yet perhaps upon the morrow
I might learn 'twas yours before,
Or some day a friend might borrow,
To return it never more!

What if I to-day should send you
Something of my very own,
No one else can give or lend you,
No one ask for on a loan—
Something that will still be waking
When the flowers in dust are strewed?
Something far too strong for breaking,
And you *can't* lose if you would.

Love I send you, very tender,
Everlasting, ever true,
That will show you how the sender
Thinks and cares and feels for you;
And when life is at its dreariest,
Or when outside things look grey,
May my fadeless present, dearest,
Point you to a brighter day!

—Harriet L. Childe-Pemberton
A Crown of Flowers, 1883, p. 24.

A Secret Way

A secret way—
'Twas made and kept for thee alone, my Love,
And never trod by man until the day
When thou didst tread its lily-beds, my Love,
And mad'st new lilies spring
When'er thy conquering footsteps fell, my
King.

A secret way—
Among its 'wildering dewy bowers, my Love,
Another but myself must go astray.
Facile to thee, the flower-grown maze, my
Love;
Of clue hast thou no need;
Straight to my heart of hearts, that way doth
lead.

—S. Alice Ranlett
Godey's Magazine, February, 1896, p. 144.

Seen, Loved, Wedded

She was a Phantom of delight
When first she gleam'd upon my sight;
A lovely Apparition, sent
To be a moment's ornament:
Her eyes as stars of twilight fair;
Like twilight's, too, her dusky hair;
But all things else about her drawn
From May-time and the cheerful Dawn;
A dancing Shape, an Image gay,
To haunt, to startle, and waylay.

I saw her upon nearer view,
A Spirit, yet a Woman too!
Her household motions light and free,
And steps of virgin liberty;
A countenance in which did meet
Sweet records, promises as sweet;
A creature not too bright or good
For human nature's daily food;
For transient sorrows, simple wiles,
Praise, blame, love, kisses, tears and smiles.

And now I see with eye serene
The very pulse of the machine;
A Being breathing thoughtful breath,
A Traveller between life and death;

The reason firm, the temperate will,
Endurance, foresight, strength, and skill;
A perfect Woman, nobly plann'd
To warn, to comfort, and command;
And yet a Spirit still, and bright
With something of an angel light.

—William Wordsworth
Fulton and Trueblood's Choice Readings, 1884.
pp. 98—99.

Ever After

When Apple Blossoms Fall

When apple blossoms fall, the sky
Is blue as southern waters are,
And fleets of cloud at anchor lie
Against the dim horizon bar;
And list the bluebird flute and call,
While bobolink pours out his tune
Through all the morn and afternoon,--
When apple blossoms fall,
And Earth's green robe about her clings,
Pinned into place by blossoms sweet
As ever bent beneath the feet,
And woodsy odored things.
When apple blossoms fall, I seem
To walk again beneath the trees,
And hear, as in a waking dream,
The sleepy drone of honey bees--
And life is love, and love is all--
It makes of Earth enchanted land
As on we loiter hand in hand,
While apple blossoms fall;
The bluebirds flute, the thrushes croon,
And through the golden afternoon

We wander on in sweet content,
With God's blue skies above us bent--
With song and bloom and sunshine blent--
In one glad symphony;
The world seems made for you and me--
And life is love, and love is all,
When apple blossoms fall.

—Anonymous
Good Housekeeping, June, 1892. p. 285.

Love's Wish

If there be a turf sweet wet
With dew and shower;
Season by season bright for some
Unfolded flower;
Where lilies in all abundance blow,
And honeysuckle and jasmine fair;
I am fain to make it the pathway where
Thy foot shall go.

If there be a breast of love
Where honour sways;
Where deep devotion knoweth not
Sour thoughts, hard ways;
If evermore this loyal breast
For some great cause beat strong and fair,
I am fain to make it the pillow where
Thy head shall rest.

If there be a love-dream quick
Wi' the rose's breath,
A dream where the heart for every day
Sweet things findeth;
A dream God blesseth verily;
Where soul with soul doth union win;
I am fain to make it the nest wherein
Thy heart shall lie.

—Emily H. Hicky, Translated from Victor Hugo
The Leisure Hour, 1891, p. 266.

A Lover's Answer

What is she like—my own, my queen of
pearls?
Like every thing God has made for long;
Like birds, and flowers, and songs, and sweet
June days.
A summer rose whose leaves have fallen
apart,
Blush after blush down to its perfect heart.
Is full of her and all her tender ways.
The cooing of a silver-throated dove
Echoes her tones; the brooklet's babbling
whirls
Mimic her laughter; showers from an April
sky
Her glistening tears. Her smiles!—ah,
evermore
On the cool bosom of the sea they lie,
And ripple, ripple, ripple to the shore.

What is she like? Like to no human thing.
The fragrant balmy breath of opening Spring
Is like her sigh; the heavy odorous air
Seems thrilling with her presence everywhere;
All the sweet luscious fruits that summer
brings
Are like her words; the butterfly's bright

wings,
Quivering in light, are radiant as her thought;
That tangled beam of yellow sunlight, caught
In dainty meshes of thin spider-lace,
Is like her warmth of hospitable grace;
The spreading branches of the tall palm-tree
Are like her all-embracing charity.

What is she like? Would I had power to tell!
Like to a sunset in its after-glow.
When all the world is dusk and dark below,
And wooded hills are clothed in misty
shrouds,
When quietly and still the waters flow,
Then the long lines of light beneath the clouds
Seem like a dream of sky beyond the skies:
In that deep hush I feel the mysteries
That hide within the shadows of her eyes,
And deeper, deeper, deeper grows the spell
As silent night above the dark earth broods,—
That heavenly night wherein her soul doth
dwell,—
Calm night the mirror of her solemn moods.

—Anonymous
Scribner's, March, 1880, p. 782.

Give Me A Rosebud

Ere summer, on unsandaled feet,
Goes, with her wealth of roses sweet,
Oh, darling one, please give to me
A rosebud, sweet and fair to see.
A lovely rose of creamy-white,
Oft kissed by shining rays of light,
And oft refreshed by gentle dew
And summer rain. Oh, dear one true,
Please let this lovely rosebud be
A token of thy love to me.
Oh, give me, dear, a rosebud fair,
That thou hast watched with tender care.
Perfect its beauty; for I know
Its loveliness would rarer grow
Beneath the gleamings of thine eyes,
Bright as the blue of sapphire skies,
A sacred treasure it will be,
A token of thy love to me.

—Aurora Vane
Peterson's Magazine, March, 1883, p. 217.

Come Find My Queen

I promised to show you my queen, did I not?
Well, follow me then, we will soon reach the
spot--
   Where unrivaled she reigns, Ah do have a
care,
   Or you surely will trip, and fall down the
stair.

What is that? you "think that these people are
queer.
   Who, their parlors have built so far in the
rear."
Well, that is your blunder not their's, you will
find,
   When we've left this long, narrow passage
behind.

For this is the kitchen, Ah yes, she is there,
My beautiful darling, so peerless and fair;
How graceful her pose amid dishes and pans,
How pleasant her smile, as some dainty she
plans.

   The curls that are nestling so close to her
brow,
   I covet the kisses they're giving her now,

I envy her apron for it doth embrace--
That form so unequaled for beauty and grace.

Unconscious of eyes that so lovingly gaze,
She is caroling one of my favorite lays.
Come away, for we have no right to play spy
I cannot exhibit her now to your eye.

But my promise I'll keep, for did I not say--
I'd show you my queen and my darling to-
day?
Ah when in the parlor her subject you've
been,
You'll say there is none can compare with my
queen.

—Ruth Argyle
Good Housekeeping, June 26, 1886. p. 100.

Lilian and I

In a snowy cottage,
With no neighbors nigh,
Live in sweet seclusion
Lilian and I

With us dwells a beauteous
Spirit from above;
In our hearts he nestles,
And his name is—Love.

—Sanda Enos
Peterson's Magazine, February, 1877, p. 111.

Content

Wonder of wonders in my stroll
I met to-day,
A woman with a loyal soul,
And deeply read in wisdom's scroll;
And I will try to tell the whole
This queen did say.

"'Tis true no carpet decks my floor,
But what of that?
God's warmest sunbeams on it pour,
And small feet through the open door
Come pit-a-pat.

"No silken webs of rare design
And tints grotesque
My windows shade; but clinging vine
And flowering plants there intertwine,
And sun and leaves and stems combine
Sweet arabesque.

"Our frugal hearth knows not the storm
That makes a part
Of many lives; our true loves form
Our brightest joys and home's sweet charms.
No fireside e'er so large can warm
A lonely heart.

"A slave? No, friend, you can not see;
You do not know.
I'd give him all; he'd all give me.
Our wills must each the other's be,
When we love most then most we're free!
This must be so.

"No sweeter, nobler lot in life
For you or me;
To be a good man's loving wife,
To guard him when temptation's rife,
Rest on his strong arm when the strife
Shall fiercest be.

"And, leaning on his faithful breast,
Look calmly out:
Secure no evil can infest,
Nor jealous fears thy peace molest;
For perfect love is perfect rest,
And dead is doubt."

I gazed upon this woman bright
In mute surprise.
I felt a coward in her sight,
I knew her glowing words were right,
Of truth the everlasting light
Was in her eyes.

—Anonymous
Good Housekeeping, March 2, 1889, p. 242.

Household Love

A little love goes very far
To smooth the daily care;
It gives a brightness to the earth,
A fragrance to the air;
A smile upon a loving face,
A word of kindness said,
This pressure of a gentle hand—
By this good work is sped,

But when a little love grows great,
And the once tiny stream
Into a glorious river spreads,
All life becomes a dream;
From neck and arms the burden falls,
We're glad and swift and strong;
We grasp our duty's hardest stroke,
And clench it with a song.

Then think, dear love, whom changeful years,
Have changeless bound to me,
How in the daily round of toil,
My feet shall bouyant be;
I cannot wish my work were less,
Your love could scarce be more;
Swift labor sings within our home
And strong love keeps the door.

—Gertrude H. Barlow
Peterson's Magazine, September, 1877, p. 210.

By the Ingle Glow

All stormy gray the width of sky
That arches o'er a world of snow;
Cold blows the wind and night is nigh;
But side by side Dear Heart and I
Sit by the ruddy ingle glow,
Love in our thoughts, love in our looks,
And worlds at arms-reach just in books.

I lean within my easy-chair
And list the while she plays and sings.
The ingle's red falls on her hair
And weaves a mystic halo there.
Ah, never all the line of kings
Held sweeter princess, dearer throne,
Than I to-night can claim my own!

We open at some witching page
Of gallant tourney long gone by;
Or con the deeds of golden age!
Or live with martyr, saint, or sage;
Or climb beneath an Alpine sky,
And chatting over prose and rhyme
So while away the happy time.

No gray clouds dim our wedded sight,
Life's eventide is far away,

So blow, O winds of darling night,
And scatter o'er the world's cold white
Your threatened freight, O storm-clouds gray,
Dear Heart and I no ill do know
Here by our ruddy ingle glow.

—Mary Clark Huntings
Good Housekeeping, March 16, 1889, p. 222.

Beautiful Hands

Oh; your hands, they are strangely fair,—
Fair for the jewels that sparkle there,
Fair for the witchery of the spell
That ivory keys alone can tell;
But when their delicate touches rest
Here in my own, I love them best,
And I clasp with eager, acquisitive spans
My glorious treasure of beautiful hands.

Marvellous, wonderful, beautiful hands,
They can coax roses to bloom in the strands
Of your brown tresses; and ribbons will twine
Under mysterious touches of thine
Into such knots as entangle the soul
And fetter the heart under such a control
As only the strength of my love understands
My passionate love for your beautiful hands.

—Anonymous
Good Housekeeping, December 24, 1887. p. 106.

Why?

I cannot tell you why I love you.
Ask the dewdrop on the rose
Why it falls and rests so softly,
Ere the lovely leaves unclose.

I cannot tell you why I love you.
Ask the bird who sweetly sings
Why he trills his tender carol,
List the answer which he brings.

I cannot tell you why I love you.
Love were lost if it could speak.
But your voice is as the bird-song,
As the dewy rose your cheek.

—Minnie C. Ballard
Peterson's Magazine, June, 1883, p. 499.

My Lady Fair

She walks in the garden, my lady fair,
With a nameless grace and a presence rare;
With rapture I gaze on her lovely face,
For all that is pure and true I trace.

She walks in the garden, my lady fair.
There's a glint of gold in her rippling hair,
She's trilling a lay of the olden time,
And her eye grows bright as her glance meets
mine.

I love her! I love her! This lady fair,
With the gracious mien and the presence rare.
And the dearest of all life's joys, I ween,
Is to call my lady my wife, my queen.

—Mrs. Pidsley
Peterson's Magazine, March, 1883, p. 239.

As In A Glass

Dear, hast thou ever learned to thy surprise
On entering a chamber mirror-lined,
That all the friends thou didst appear to find
Were but thyself reflected several wise?
The room seemed full to unaccustomed eyes
Whilst thou wert there; but when thou wert
inclined
To leave it, nothing then remained behind.
But emptiness, proportioned to its size.
So if thou lookest in my heart, dear Love,
Such overflowing fullness wilt thou see
That thou shalt seek a vacant spot in vain:
But on close inspection it will prove
To be completely filled with naught but
thee—
And wert thou gone, then nothing would
remain.

—Ellen Thorneycroft Fowler
The Leisure Hour, 1891, p. 164.

Song

As birds soar high
In the charmèd sky,
And far from earth exulting fly,
My love to you,
Which is old and new,
Wings away through the gray and blue
Of wintry skies between us two.

Both new and old
Is this love I fold
Deep and safe away from the cold.
Not old, you say!
Dear heart, each day,
Though skies be blue, though skies be gray,
Older it grows, yet new alway.

—Anonymous
Harper's New Monthly Magazine, April, 1884, p. 671.

Courtship or Marriage?

Marriage is an ordered garden,
Courtship, a sweet tangled wood;
Marriage is the sober Summer,
Courtship, Spring, in wayward mood;
Marriage is a deep, still river,
Courtship, a bright laughing stream;
Marriage is a dear possesssion,
Courtship, a perplexing dream:
Which of these, my wife, shall be
Crowned as best by thee and me?

Marriage is a blue day's beauty,
Courtship, the capricious morn;
Marriage is the sweet Rose gathered,
Courtship, but still fenced with thorn;
Marriage is the pearl in setting,
Courtship is the dangerous dive;
Marriage the full comb of honey,
Courtship, the new-buzzing hive:
—Which of these, dear wife, shall be
First preferred by thee and me?

O, the tangled wood was lovely,
When we found it, in our play,
Parting curiously the branches
White with masses of the May,

Eagerly the paths exploring
Leading to we knew not where,
Save that million flowers edged them,
And that bird-songs lit the air,
Thrushes' joy-notes, Philomela's
Still more exquisite despair.

How we wandered!—Now our wild wood
Has become a garden plot,
Something missed of that strange sweetness,
In the method of our lot.
—Ordered walks, and formal borders
For the wood-paths strange and wild,
Rose superb, and stately lily,
Where the careless wood flowers smiled,
—Summer, grave and sober matron,
For young Spring, the eager child;
Which, O which perferred shall be,
Twelve-years' wife, by me and thee?

Nay, the garden has its glory,
Stately flower and fruit mature;
And the wild wood had its dearness,
Strange delights and wonders pure;
And the summer has fulfillment,
If the spring has promise-store;
And the river is the deeper,
If the young brook laugheth more;
And the real joy abideth,

When the teasing dreams are o'er.

And the broad blue sky has glories,
If the morn was wildly fair;
And the gathered rose is safer,
If the buds more piquant were;
And the pearl is raze and precious,
If the dive was full of glee;
And we would not change our honey,
For the flower-quest of the bee;
—Sweet is Courtship; sweet is Marriage;
Crown them, darling, equally!!

—J.R. Vernon
The Leisure Hour, 1891, p. 254.

113

Index of Titles

Index of First Lines

Printed in Great Britain
by Amazon

21437516R00072